W9-BRJ-687

NORTH HAVEN
MEMORIAL LIBRARY
NORTH HAVEN, CONNECTICUT

CHRISTOPHER
COLUMBUS

North Haven Memorial Library
North Haven, CT 06473

CHRISTOPHER COLUMBUS

Copyright © 1987, Raintree Publishers Limited Partnership

All rights reserved. No part of this book may be reproduced
or utilized in any form or by any means, electronic or mechanical,
including photocopying, recording, or by any information storage
and retrieval system, without permission in writing from the
Publisher. Inquiries should be addressed to Raintree Publishers,
310 W. Wisconsin Avenue, Milwaukee, Wisconsin 53203.

Library of Congress Number: 86-20387

2 3 4 5 6 7 8 9 10   99 98 97 96 95 94 93 92 91 90

Library of Congress Cataloging in Publication Data

Gleiter, Jan, 1947-
  Christopher Columbus.

  (Raintree stories)
  Summary: Presents the life of the fifteenth-
century explorer and how he came to discover the
New World.
   1. Columbus, Christopher—Juvenile literature.
2. Explorers—America—Biography—Juvenile literature.
3. Explorers—Spain—Biography—Juvenile literature.
4. America—Discovery and exploration—Spanish—
Juvenile literature.   [1. Columbus, Christopher.
2. Explorers]I. Thompson, Kathleen.   II. Whipple,
Rick, ill.   III. Title.
E111.G55   1986   970.01′5 [B] [92]   86-20387
ISBN 0-8172-2643-5 (lib. bdg.)
ISBN 0-8172-2647-8 (softcover)

CHRISTOPHER COLUMBUS

Jan Gleiter and Kathleen Thompson

Illustrated by Rick Whipple

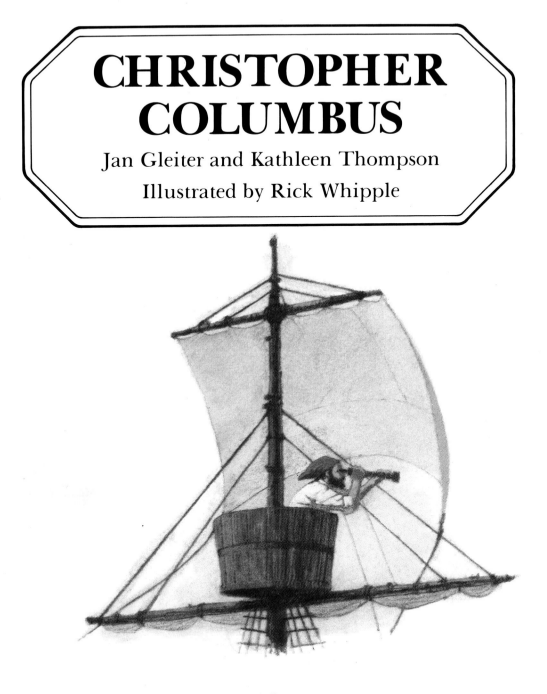

Raintree Publishers
Milwaukee

The boy stood high up in the ship's rigging. He was, as usual, looking for land.

"Fernando! Boy! Roll up that sail!" The rough voice of a sailor reached his ears.

Fernando hurried to do as he was told. The sail was heavy and the boy was small. But, on this ship, boys did men's work. And they did it well. Fernando finished his job and started down the ropes.

The ship rolled suddenly. The boy swung out, his feet off the ropes. Only his tight grip saved him from a fall to the deck far below. He scrambled the rest of the way down before the ship could roll again.

As Fernando crossed the deck, he heard two other boys talking. They were angry.

"We'd be safely ashore with plenty to eat," said one, "if it weren't for that old goat, Columbus!"

The other boy laughed in a mean way. "I've heard the men talking," he said. "They're ready to do something about him. And I'm ready to join them."

Fernando stepped closer. "I wouldn't if I were you," he said sharply. "And I'd watch what I said about the admiral."

"Oh, you're tough," laughed the first boy. "Like father, like son! If you don't want the men to take over this ship, tell your father to watch his step."

Fernando went below deck. He didn't want to worry his father. But he wanted him to know what he had heard.

The admiral, Christopher Columbus, was sitting at a table, writing a letter. He listened to his son.

"You know I'm with you, Father," said the boy. "I'll fight with you if we have to."

Columbus smiled. "This isn't the first time my men have wanted a new leader," he said. "I know how to deal with them. I am glad for your offer of help. But thirteen-year-old boys shouldn't have to fight their fathers' battles."

Christopher Columbus did know how to deal with his men. The mutiny that Fernando had heard the boys talking about was not the first. But the rebels had always lost these fights, and they lost this one too.

Columbus was not an easy man to sail with. He could use the stars to steer by. He could find his way over unknown seas. He was a man of big plans, big ideas. He was brave, he was smart, and he was determined. But he had his own way of doing things, and he didn't listen to anybody else. He was probably the greatest sailor of his time. He certainly didn't think there was any doubt about that. Neither did Fernando.

Columbus loved to tell his son about his adventures on the sea and in the lands he had discovered. And Fernando loved to listen.

A few nights later, Fernando stood with his father on the deck. The only sound was the gentle creaking of the wooden ship. A cool breeze lifted his hair. He looked up at his father. "Tell me about your first voyage to the New World, Father," he asked.

"Now, let's see," said Columbus. "That was a long time ago, ten years. I don't know if I remember it well enough."

Fernando laughed. He knew his father remembered every detail of that first great voyage. After all, hadn't he been the first European to dare to cross the huge ocean? Hadn't he been the one who found a whole new world?

S tart at the beginning, Father," demanded his son. "The very beginning, when you went to the king and queen of Spain to get the money for the voyage."

"Ah," said his father. "But that wasn't the beginning. In the beginning, I went to King John of Portugal. Portugal had the greatest sailors and the best ships. I needed good men and good ships because I had an idea, a grand idea."

Y ou knew you could get to the Indies by sea," said Fernando. He knew the story well, and sometimes couldn't help interrupting.

The Indies was the name, at that time, for India, China, the East Indies, and Japan. The Indies lay far to the east and the journey there by land was long and hard. But the Indies were rich in gold, spices, silk, and jewels. Everyone wanted a quicker way to get there.

"Yes," his father went on. "I was quite sure of it. I had studied the situation. I knew the best, the fastest and best, way to get to the East was to sail . . ."

"West!" shouted Fernando.

Yes," agreed his father. He touched his son's right ear. "This," he said, "is Europe." He touched his son's left ear. "And this is the Indies. Now, I could walk and walk east across all this land. . ." He traced his finger across Fernando's nose. "Or, because the world is round, I could sail the other way, west." He drew his hand across the back of Fernando's head and grabbed his left ear.

"Ah, ha! The Indies! Just as I thought!"

B ut King John didn't believe you?" asked his son.

"Oh, he knew the world was round," said Columbus. "Most everyone understood that. But King John had experts. These experts thought they knew more than anyone about the sea and where the Indies could be found."

Fernando nodded. "And the king listened to them, not to you."

That's right," agreed his father. "He listened to them." Suddenly he let out a roar of laughter and slapped the deck rail. "And I bet they're kicking themselves all over Portugal now!"

"And maybe the king gave them a boot in the pants too, when he heard what you'd done," said Fernando. His eyes were shining.

"Oh, you never know," said Columbus. "You never know about kings. Or queens for that matter." For a moment, his voice was bitter.

"So you went to King Ferdinand and Queen Isabella of Spain," said his son. "And then?"

Then I went to them again. And again," said Columbus. "I drew maps for them. I argued. I begged. They thought I wanted too much money and too much power. Ha! I was the one taking the risk! But they finally agreed. I set sail with three ships and ninety men in August of 1492."

"And you sailed and sailed," said Fernando, with a dreamy look in his eyes. "On the Niña, the Pinta, and the Santa Maria."

"And I sailed and sailed," agreed his father. "And then I sailed some more. The men were eager at first. But when the weeks went by with no sight of land, they got scared. The wind kept blowing us west, and they thought we'd never find a wind to bring us home again."

The ship rocked gently on the water. Columbus looked up at the stars twinkling in the dark sky.

"Finally I told them we would turn back in three days if we hadn't found land. I had no choice. I knew the land was there. I knew it! But there had already been one mutiny that had almost beaten me. I couldn't sleep, couldn't do anything but hope. And then . . ."

"Land!" said Fernando.

"No," murmured his father. His eyes were soft with memory. "Birds. All night we heard them passing. In the morning, we saw them. Flocks of birds, all flying toward the southwest. So I ordered the ships to change course. We followed the birds, southwest."

Fernando couldn't wait. "And then, late at night," he whispered, "while no one could sleep, a lookout shouted, 'Land!'"

"Yes," sighed Columbus. "Land, at last. And it wasn't just any land we saw that night in the moonlight. It was a heaven on earth, a new world."

"We went ashore," he went on. "And the people who lived there met us and gave us gifts. I named the place San Salvador."

The "Indies" that Columbus had found were not the Indies at all. He believed he was just off the shores of China or Japan. But he had landed in the Bahama Islands, southeast of Florida. He never realized how wrong he was. He never realized that he had really landed on the edge of an entire continent that Europe knew nothing about. He had done something far greater than he had imagined.

Columbus looked out over the water. "I claimed San Salvador for Spain, and found many more islands to claim. On Christmas Eve that same year, we ran aground on a reef and lost the Santa Maria."

"And you almost didn't make it home. Isn't that right, Father?"

"I was sure we wouldn't make it home," said his father. "The storms on our way back were so bad that I wrote down the story of my discoveries. I sealed the papers in a wooden cask and threw it overboard. My greatest fear was not death. It was that no one would know what I had found."

ut you did make it home to Spain," said Fernando. He knew this part of the story very well, the part that told of his father's glory. "And the king and queen listened to all that had happened, all you had done! They made you an admiral, Admiral of the Ocean Sea! And now we're going back to that New World."

"Yes," agreed his father. "We're going back. I have been there twice already. But you, my son, you will see for yourself now what I saw for the first time ten years ago."

"And I shall find gold to take home to Spain," said the boy, his face eager. "And you shall make new discoveries!"

Before that trip was over, Christopher Columbus put down more mutinies, fought with the natives, and searched for shelter and food. He and his men lived through storms that tossed their ships like matchsticks on the rolling sea. Those ships were finally lost, ruined by the holes eaten in them by shipworms.

But Columbus and his men made it home again. And many years later, Fernando would write about the voyage and about his father, Christopher Columbus, Admiral of the Ocean Sea.

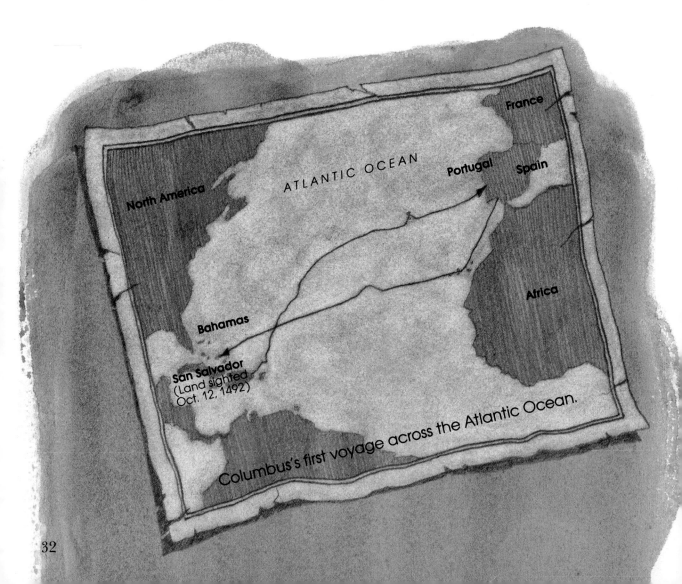

Columbus's first voyage across the Atlantic Ocean.